The Friendly Beasts

A CHRISTMAS CAROL
ILLUSTRATED
BY Sharon McGinley

Greenwillow Books

An Imprint of HarperCollins*Publishers*

The Friendly Beasts

Special thanks to Ann Pierson

Gouache was used for the full-color art.
The text type is Meridien.

The song lyrics are from
"The Friendly Beasts" by Robert Davis.

The Friendly Beasts
Illustrations © 2000 by Sharon McGinley
Arrangement © 2000 by David Wolff
All rights reserved.
Printed in Singapore by Tien Wah Press.
www.harperchildrens.com

Library of Congress Cataloging-in-Publication Data
McGinley-Nally, Sharon.
The friendly beasts / Sharon McGinley.
    p.   cm.
"Greenwillow Books."
Summary: In this version of a traditional
Christmas carol, the friendly stable beasts
tell of the gifts they have given to the
newborn Jesus.
ISBN 0-688-17421-3 (trade).
ISBN 0-688-17422-1 (lib. bdg.)
1. Carols, English—Texts.
2. Christmas music—Texts.
[l. Carols. 2. Christmas music.]
I. Title.
PZ8.3.M1575 Fr 2000   782.28'1723—dc21
99-033704

1 2 3 4 5 6 7 8 9 10 First Edition

For Leo

Jesus our Brother, kind and good,

Was humbly born in a stable rude,

And the friendly beasts around Him stood.

Jesus our Brother, kind and good.

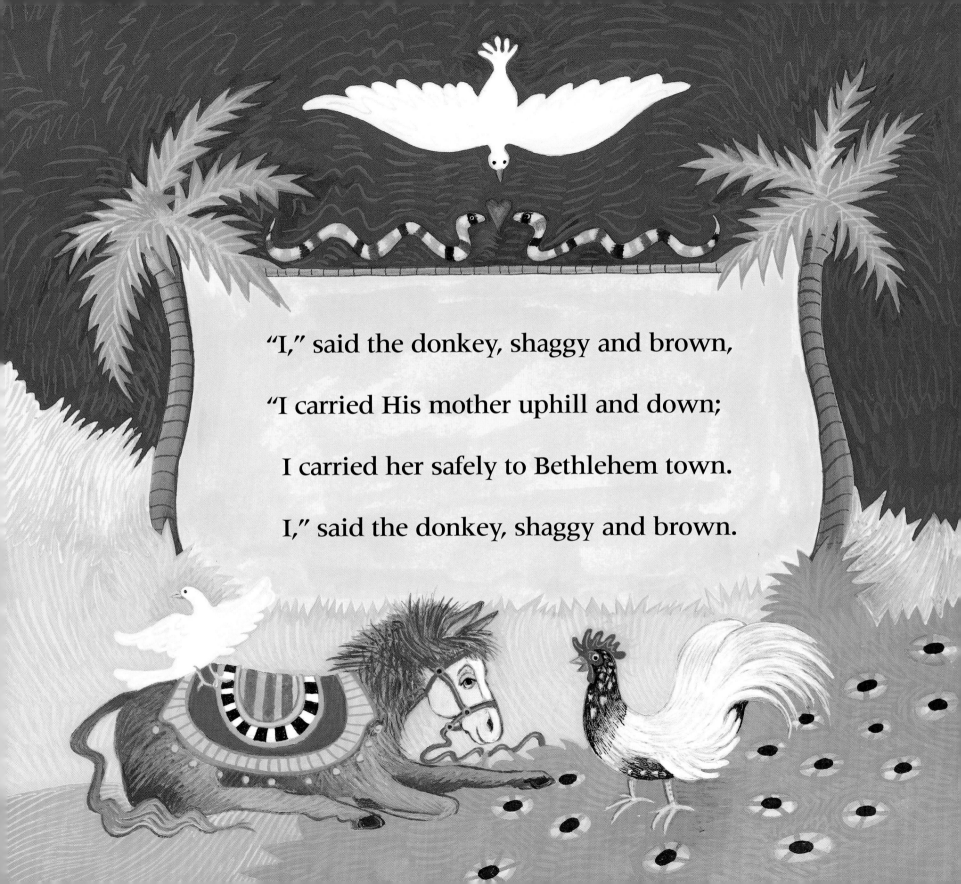

"I," said the donkey, shaggy and brown,

"I carried His mother uphill and down;

I carried her safely to Bethlehem town.

I," said the donkey, shaggy and brown.

"I," said the cow, all white and red,

"I gave Him my manger for His bed;

I gave Him my hay to pillow His head.

I," said the cow, all white and red.

"I," said the sheep with the curly horn,

"I gave Him my wool for a blanket warm;

He wore my coat on Christmas morn.

I," said the sheep with the curly horn.

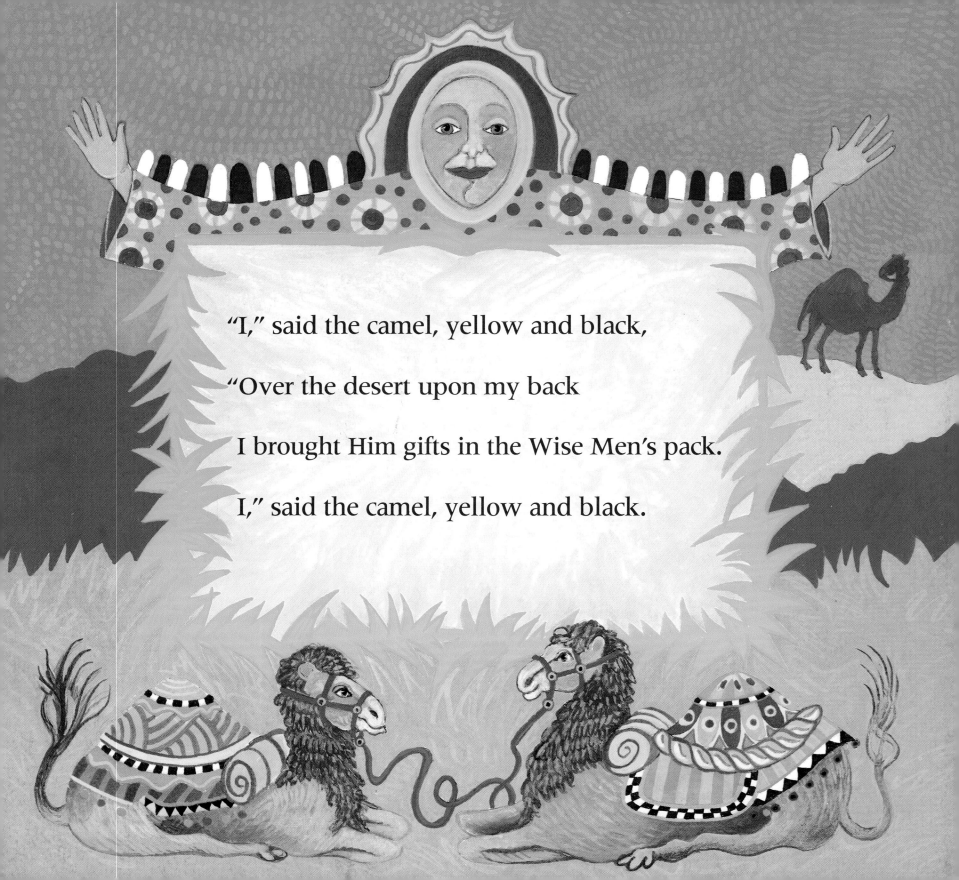

"I," said the camel, yellow and black,

"Over the desert upon my back

I brought Him gifts in the Wise Men's pack.

I," said the camel, yellow and black.

"I," said the dove, from the rafters high,

"I cooed Him to sleep so He would not cry;

We cooed Him to sleep, my mate and I.

I," said the dove, from the rafters high.

THUS EVERY BEAST BY SOME GOOD SPELL,

IN THE STABLE DARK WAS GLAD TO TELL

OF THE GIFTS THEY GAVE EMMANUEL,

THE GIFTS THEY GAVE EMMANUEL.

The Friendly Beasts

Words: Robert Davis

Music: Traditional French
Arrangement: David Wolff

2. "I," said the donkey, shaggy and brown,
   "I carried His mother uphill and down;
   I carried her safely to Bethlehem town.
   I," said the donkey, shaggy and brown.

3. "I," said the cow, all white and red,
   "I gave Him my manger for His bed;
   I gave Him my hay to pillow His head.
   I," said the cow, all white and red.

4. "I," said the sheep with the curly horn,
   "I gave Him my wool for a blanket warm;
   He wore my coat on Christmas morn.
   I," said the sheep with the curly horn.

5. "I," said the camel, yellow and black,
   "Over the desert upon my back
   I brought Him gifts in the Wise Men's pack.
   I," said the camel, yellow and black.

6. "I," said the dove, from the rafters high,
   "I cooed Him to sleep so He would not cry;
   We cooed Him to sleep, my mate and I.
   I," said the dove, from the rafters high.

7. Thus every beast by some good spell,
   In the stable dark was glad to tell
   Of the gifts they gave Emmanuel,
   The gifts they gave Emmanuel.

A NOTE ON "THE FRIENDLY BEASTS"

"The Friendly Beasts" is a Christmas carol with an identity crisis. Its tune is very old, a twelfth-century French, or possibly English, melody entitled "Orientis Partibus," which means "Eastern Lands." It was traditionally sung at Christmastime for a religious feast called the Donkey's Festival, a re-enactment of Joseph and Mary's flight to Egypt with the baby Jesus. During the festival a donkey, adorned with the colors of the rainbow, carried a woman and baby through the streets, while a procession followed, singing in Latin the words:

"From Eastern lands comes the Donkey,
Beautiful and strong Donkey,
Most patient carrier of burdens.
Hee-haw, Sir Donkey, hee-haw!"

Though many hymnals and carol books mistakenly label the words to "The Friendly Beasts" as "Medieval French" or "Traditional," they actually were written in the twentieth century by an American. The imaginative lyrics by Robert Davis were copyrighted in 1920, and they appear in no songbook before 1934. Very little is known about Davis himself, and unfortunately he is rarely given credit for transforming an ancient festival song into the modern children's classic about the animals who brought gifts to the Christ child.